HOW DO YOU KNOW WHAT TIME IT IS?

Robert E. Wells

Albert Whitman & Company · Morton Grove, Illinois

For my parents-in-law, Jess and Lavaun Dunning, who have invested much of *their* time promoting peace and justice.

Library of Congress Cataloging-in-Publication Data

Wells, Robert E.
How do you know what time it is? / written and illustrated
by Robert E. Wells.
p.   cm.
ISBN 0-8075-7939-4 (hardcover)
ISBN 0-8075-7940-8 (pbk.)
1. Time measurements. I. Title.
QB213 .W46   2002   2002001954
529' .7—dc21   CIP
                                              AC

Hand-lettering by Robert E. Wells.
The illustration media are pen and acrylic.
Design by Susan B. Cohn.

Also by Robert E. Wells
Can You Count to a Googol?
How Do You Lift a Lion?
Is a Blue Whale the Biggest Thing There Is?
What's Faster Than a Speeding Cheetah?
What's Smaller Than a Pygmy Shrew?

TIME is a mystery.
You can't *see* it. You can't *hear* it.
You can't catch it in a net and put it in a jar.
But you know time is real because you
can sense it passing by.

In a way, time is like the wind.

You can't see the wind, but you can see what happens when it blows.

Kites fly in the air,

clouds move across the sky,

and boats sail over the water.

And you can see what happens when time passes.
Blossoms turn into apples,

cubs grow up to be bears,

and caterpillars become butterflies.

But time is more mysterious than the wind. It's so mysterious that even the greatest thinkers and scientists can't say exactly what it is!

Even so, it's a mystery we can measure.

Not with a measuring tape, of course. That's what you'd use to measure an alligator!

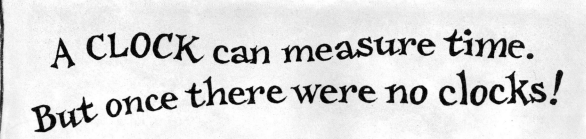

Long long ago, people measured time with the sun.

By observing the sun's position as it moved across the sky, early people could tell how much time they had to gather food or firewood before darkness returned.

Our ancestors didn't know why the sun kept appearing and disappearing.

They didn't understand, as we do today, that Earth is round and turns like a top,

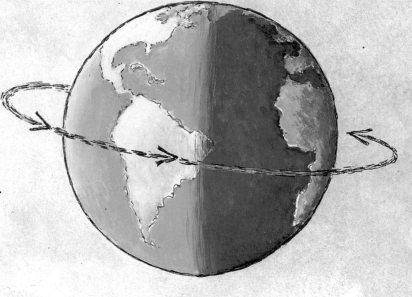

so that the world is light where it faces the sun and dark where it faces away.

After a while, people invented simple time-measuring devices.

Egyptians made SHADOW STICK clocks. As the sun moved across the sky, the stick's shadow moved around stone markers.

At night they used WATER CLOCKS. Water dripped from one pot to another pot with marks inside to measure time.

DRIP DRIP
DRIP DRIP
DRIP
DRIP

Egyptians were among the first to divide time into hours.

In Europe, SUNDIALS measured hours more accurately than shadow sticks,

and SANDGLASSES measured time with falling sand.

FALLING WEIGHT TURNS CLOCK GEARS

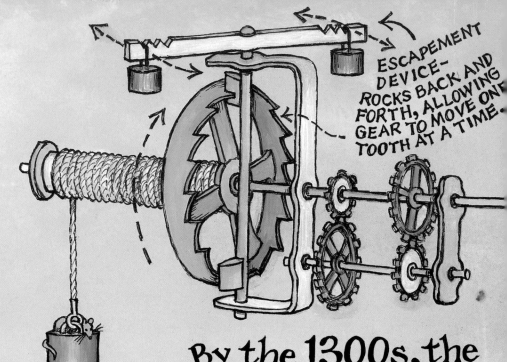

ESCAPEMENT DEVICE— ROCKS BACK AND FORTH, ALLOWING GEAR TO MOVE ONE TOOTH AT A TIME.

By the 1300s, the MECHANICAL CLOCK measured time with gears and weights.

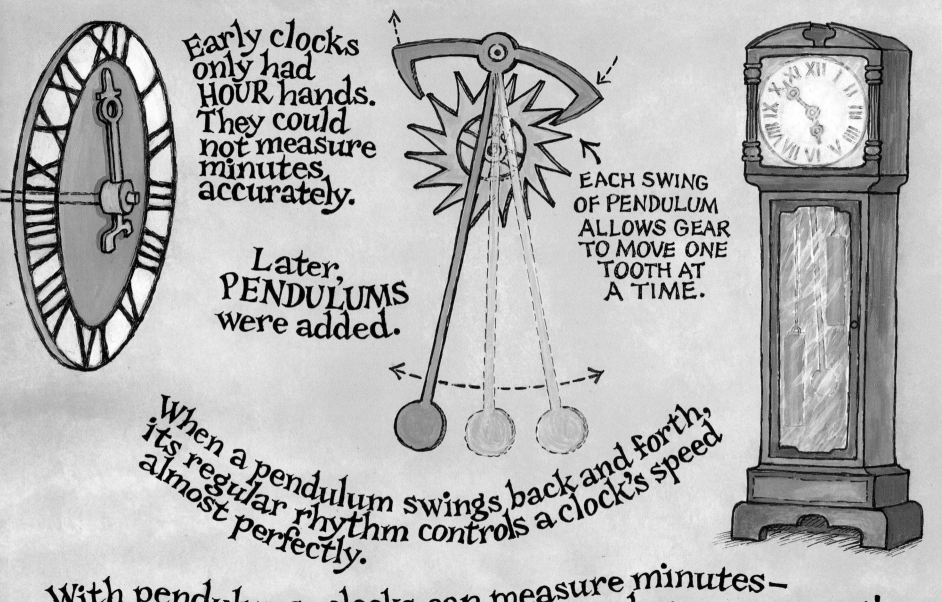

Early clocks only had HOUR hands. They could not measure minutes accurately.

Later, PENDULUMS were added.

EACH SWING OF PENDULUM ALLOWS GEAR TO MOVE ONE TOOTH AT A TIME.

When a pendulum swings back and forth, its regular rhythm controls a clock's speed almost perfectly.

With pendulums, clocks can measure minutes— and even SECONDS!

While the sun helped early people measure a day, the moon's changing shape helped them keep track of MONTHS.

FULL

NEW

In Egypt, the regular flooding of the Nile River was very important because the water brought new soil to the fields.

Egyptians began to keep track of the time between new moons to help them predict when the next flood would come.

Long ago, people didn't know why the moon changed shape. Today we know why. As the moon orbits, or travels around, Earth, it's always half-lit by our sun, as shown. But from Earth, we see that light from different angles, causing the different shapes.

SUN'S LIGHT CAUSES MOON TO ALWAYS BE HALF LIGHT, HALF DARK.

SHAPE WE SEE FROM EARTH.

It takes about 29½ days for the moon to change through all its shapes as it orbits once around Earth. We call that the MOON CYCLE.

The Egyptians saw that about 12 moon cycles passed between each flood. They made LUNAR CALENDARS, dividing 12 moon cycles into 3 SEASONS: Flooding, Planting, and Harvest.

But they soon discovered they had to add extra days to the calendars, because 12 moon cycles are 11 days shorter than the cycle of the seasons, or one year.

The Egyptians didn't know why the moon cycles didn't match the seasons.

Today we know that our seasons are not measured by the moon, but by Earth's orbit of the SUN!

As Earth travels around the sun, it revolves on an imaginary line called an AXIS.

Earth's axis is tipped at an angle.

This causes the part of Earth that's tipped toward the sun to be warmer, and the part that's tipped *away* to be cooler.

The changing amount of sunlight causes the changes in our seasons.

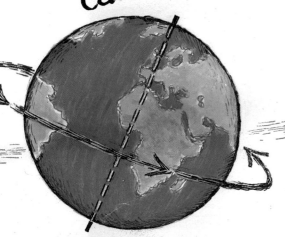

It takes about 365¼ days for Earth to orbit the sun. We call that a SOLAR YEAR.

Later, the Egyptians began to use a SOLAR CALENDAR. They knew that the star Sirius always made its first appearance in the morning sky just before the floods. So, they chose that day to begin each year.

Since Sirius is in this position only once during Earth's orbit, the new calendar measured the year at 365 days - just ¼ of a day short!

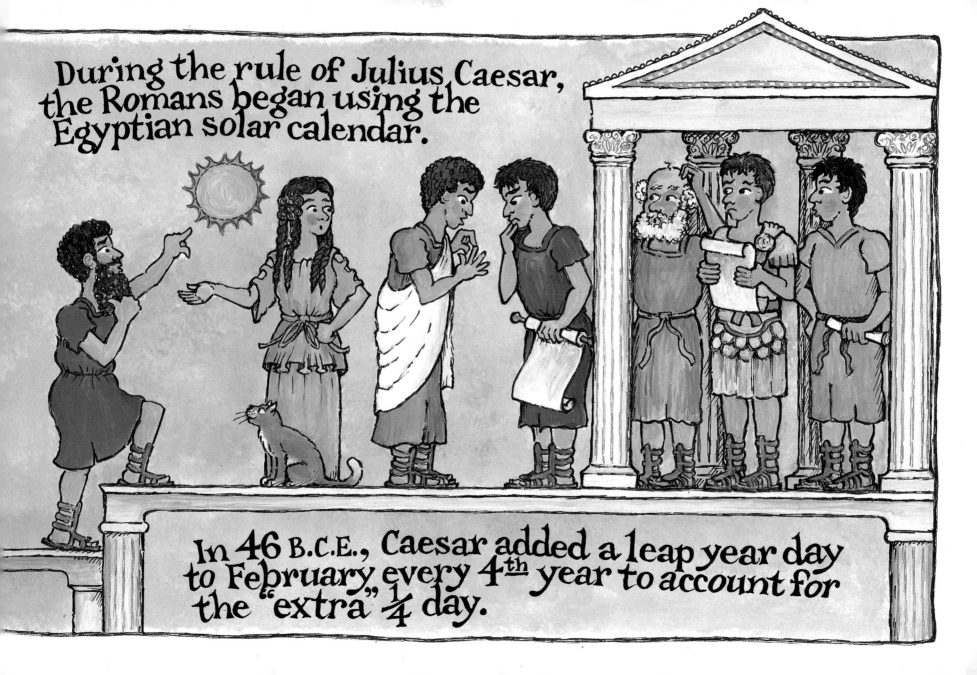

During the rule of Julius Caesar, the Romans began using the Egyptian solar calendar.

In 46 B.C.E., Caesar added a leap year day to February every 4th year to account for the "extra" $\frac{1}{4}$ day.

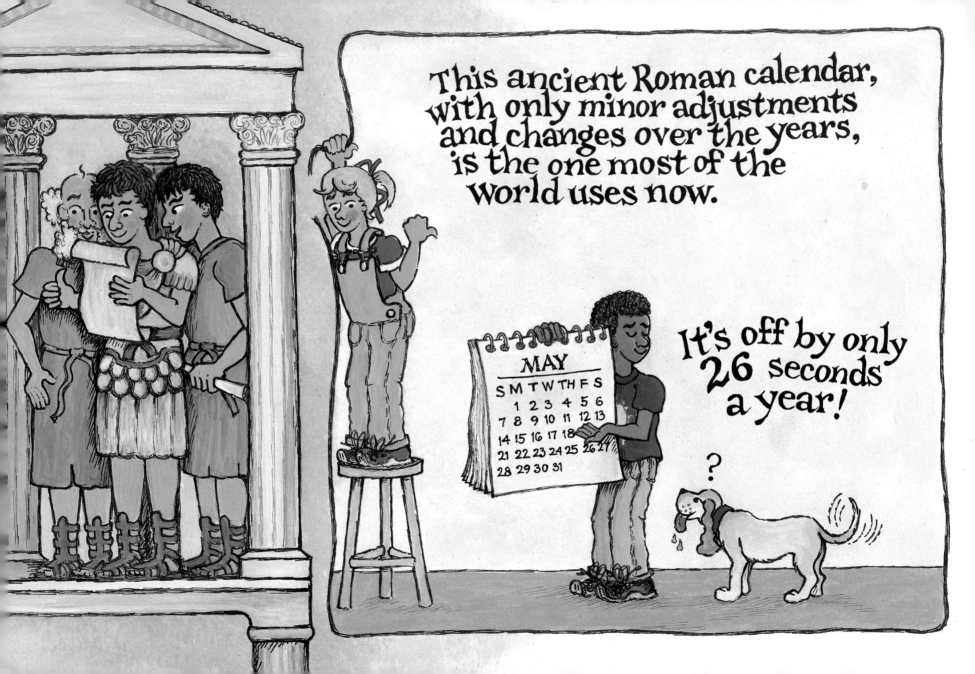

Today our calendar is almost perfect, and with atomic clocks, we can know the exact time anywhere on Earth! But because it's DAYtime on one side of Earth while it's NIGHTtime on the other,

it would be confusing if clocks around the world showed the same time.

Some people would be eating lunch in the dark!

To solve that problem, our world has been divided into 24 TIME ZONES, one hour apart, and centered on MERIDIAN lines.

With time zones, it's not the same time for everyone.

TIME ZONE

1 P.M. 2 P.M. 3 P.M. 4 P.M. 5 P.M. 6 P.M. 7 P.M. 8 P.M. 9 P.M. 10 P.M. 11

Time zones usually follow the meridian lines, but sometimes zigzag around cities or countries to avoid dividing them.

TIME ZONE DIVIDING LINE.

9 A.M.

10 A.M.

If you straddle the line dividing 2 zones, it could be 9 A.M. for your right foot and 10 A.M. for your left foot!

LOS ANGELES

NEW YORK

-R-R-R-RING-G-G-G

And if you're in Los Angeles at 9 P.M., you'd better not call a friend in New York for a chat— It's *midnight* there!

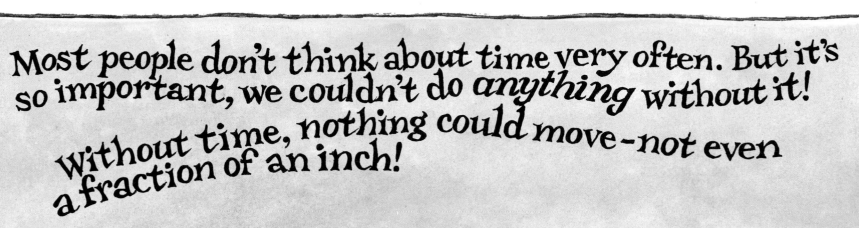

Most people don't think about time very often. But it's so important, we couldn't do *anything* without it!

Without time, nothing could move—not even a fraction of an inch!

You couldn't even blink your eyes.

No matter how fast you blinked, it would take a tiny bit of time!

WITHOUT TIME PASSING BY, you couldn't play a computer game or eat a bowl of ice cream or paint a picture or ski down a slope.

How *could you?* All those things take TIME!

Time Marches On!

Until the seventeenth century, the SUNDIAL was our most accurate timekeeper; then its accuracy was surpassed by the PENDULUM CLOCK.

In the early twentieth century, scientists discovered that when electricity is applied to a plate, or slice, of a QUARTZ CRYSTAL, the plate vibrates at an exact rate. Now it was possible to make small timepieces that were even more accurate than pendulum clocks.

ATOMIC CLOCKS, counting the vibrations of cesium atoms, were invented in the mid-twentieth century. Atomic clocks are much more accurate than quartz crystal clocks, and are now Earth's official timekeepers.

TIME ZONES make it possible to have one standard time for everyone in a particular zone. By an international agreement made in 1884, the first zone, or PRIME MERIDIAN, passes through England. West of the prime meridian, each zone is one hour earlier, and east, one hour later. On the other side of the world is the INTERNATIONAL DATE LINE, which is the 180th meridian. By crossing this line, a traveler goes from one day to another.

Today, no matter where on Earth you go, there's one thing you can count on: our world is always right on time!